Dead Bolt

Dead Bolt

Ella Jeffery

PUNCHER & WATTMANN

First published in 2020
Published by Puncher and Wattmann
PO Box 279
Waratah NSW 2298

http://www.puncherandwattmann.com
puncherandwattmann@bigpond.com

NATIONAL
LIBRARY
OF AUSTRALIA

A catalogue entry for this book is available from the National Library of Australia.

ISBN   9781925780710

Cover design by Miranda Douglas

Printed by Lightning Source International

Contents

1

In the former French Concession

I see them from my bedroom,
pegged beside the neighbour's
smog-coloured slips,
and on street corners
in the black thatch of power lines:
fish dried crisp, leaf-print bodies
honed to bone,
mined for eyes and eggs,
scales and fins mixed
in the gutter with other rubbish,
fish winched between drying ducks
round as spuds, rich with flesh,
bronze fish jangling above tourists,
causing arguments between neighbours,
taut in the wind, fish
big as tables, headless fish,
fish curved and smooth as boat hulls,
split and spread flat like sails
turning white in the white weather,
wearing a crest of frost.

Above me in the former French Concession
several small fish on the wire ravel
of a coathanger, flesh cured
of saltiness, unscented as soap,
beside themselves in the wet market
rows and rows of brineless silence,
last night's meal needled
with bones, on Jiashan Road
those that have dried their time are for sale,
the new twisting over footpaths
still tiled with scales,
eyes cataracted by cloud,

pious and quiet,
kids in a fish-trance
staring up into the silver dizziness
fish bones scattered like scratch marks
where cats get fed,
in the entrance to my apartment
two little fish
hang
in the window
like neighbours' faces.

Simon Schama's *The Power of Art*

An Englishman is playing sweaty Caravaggio on TV
and Simon narrates in the historical present:
Caravaggio paints—
paints himself to death (exaggeration)
runs, struggles, dies on a beach,
running after a boat
in the blue distance that's sketching off to Rome
with his last paintings (maybe).

Six o'clock darkness steers
the room away from time
and place. It could be any day:
maybe if I open the door I will see myself
in the kitchen, preparing yesterday's breakfast;
or talking, three months ago,
about leaving Shanghai for good;
in the next room
it is last year and I am yawing
in sleep across my shipwrecked sheets.
Perhaps it's lucky I'm still here
in these rooms
in the present tense.

Fragment: Tuesday evening, Waitan

Just looking, I say
to the man selling cups and cutlery
from a pushcart parked
by the Huangpu.
He says it back: just looking,
rolls out the vowels like a spare mattress,
a foreigner's hazy phrase.
We hassle each other over prices
and I take the two cups I've chosen
for their colour. Behind us,
white light scrapes the river
where a coal boat
murmurs to the coast
like a child with half
her face in the water.

Sam reads the *Iliad*

This morning he raises
the bronze wreck
of his face
when I drift in, then pitches
back to the book.

He has ground hours over
these pages, gripping
the kitchen bench
as though the floor's an edge
he might slide off.

The day crumbles. I want
to mewl in the dark turf
of his body while he worries
over violence and entropy

or untwists hexameter
but he is vacant
as stone. I sift
through his notebook half-asleep,
sweat out a fever
of sudden dreams.

Nothing damages that book.
Not his spilled coffee or the lesser
pollens of his body,
dandruff, quick
of his fingers clawing
the red-flecked burrs on his face.

Not history grinding
its molars

while I wake and sleep
in a creel of wrenched bedsheets.

Language immersion programs and their benefits

I threw out a wok scabbed
greenwhite as a boat hull
and a ceiling fan
lying like a dead dragonfly,
a smash of angles.

Kept the bible in Mandarin
and guidebooks in French
as if I could flip through the years
and get back one language
or learn the other. I fanned them
under the glasstop table
where they crazed my eyes
whenever I entered the room.

Nothing is entirely wrecked or lost.
My neighbours know this.
Their brilliant and invisible cooking
skims into my bedroom
some nights.

What will I ask them when I stumble
into speech—how did they scour
that barnacled wok and what
might still happen to us all,
in this building matted
with scaffolding,
their kitchen hung open like a mouth.

Smart animals

He is the dog's boss, lǎo bǎn, clan chief of all stray cats
and humans he feeds. In Avranches I saw him wolf
the plate of intestines I ordered by mistake, while I nuzzled
mussels in sweet sauce. In Gatton he trained clever mutts
to wear armour and crunch beside him through scrub,
hunted boars with a long knife when I was still a child,
feeding my goldfish its per diem of flakes. He is born again
every morning naked and uncertain, in many places
at once, until the world shears back into view. He remembers me
and his pupil swims close in its tea-tree pool.
Perhaps what he loves best are belligerent devotions,
his old cockatoo who strafes the ear all day
for his nearness, then nips the finger offered through the cage.
But still he offers it, gave the bird a name. He was born
with a mouth full of names to give out: he has the right word
when I want to describe a roundish fish with rainbows
mangled in its gills, or a dog riffling through muck
on the street – smart animals, he says, but difficult to train.
And if I need the name of a beach-dwelling tree, he gifts me
a pandanus, spiked like the first earthly pleasure.

Quotient

It's not difficult to work out
the number of times
one quantity is contained
in another and sometimes
there is no remainder
and that zero,
that nothing, is a gift

in the same way that sitting
alone in a busy park
where everyone speaks
a language you cannot understand
is to touch the edges of silence
and feel it seal perfectly around you.

Mutianyu in June

Clouds in the west
tinged the freak green of hail.

There was nobody around.
I walked for hours along the wall

and now and then I'd run
into other people in twos or threes.

We nodded at each other in our plastic
raincoats. For ten minutes

I watched a wild donkey
stand in the rain

among the trees below.
Fog pulsed through watchtowers.

Sometimes the steps
were far bigger and further

apart than I am used to.
Sometimes they were so small

and steep I lifted my whole
body on the balls of my feet

and laid my hands
on the rain-slick steps

above and pulled myself upwards,
grazing stone with my knees

and ankles and shins, bones
I thought I had outgrown.

Blackout

The clock's gone off.
I watch it throw
empty eights while I curdle
in sweat-wet sheets. You are awake
in the deviceless silence,
microwaving a slice of frozen bread
stilled
on its yellow plate.

In the egg-ring of torchlight
when we come outside:
thongs curled like fossils
by the back steps,
one huntsman I tread to death.
I kick away its body
so you and I don't fight.
I'll slaughter them
until there are none left alive
and the ecosystem crumples
like butcher's paper. Then—

the porch light sharpens
its little white knife
and carves our shadows in the grass.
No voice streaks out
from any neighbour's house.
I ask *was it just us*
as if you speak
for the wires that circuit this street.

Brunoise

There is no smell to her. She is candlewax and a cake-batter
spatter of freckles. She holds the stick blender and witches
up a red wreck of berries that she says makes her body strong.
Which is no lie: she lifted the washing machine when something
went wrong and I fishtailed in the kitchen. Everything
she owns is sharp and in sets: Wüsthof knives in a cream
woodblock, shoulder blades that could make a julienned mess
of her taffy bedspread or her pink-and-white dress. She hums
all afternoon in one room or another, knows the exact dimensions
of a standard dishwasher, came to live here one rainy weekend.
In the evening she is pastel, some nights the frenzied gold
of treasure by torchlight, sometimes fruit-soft, sometimes pliant,
sometimes Laminex-white, knife-tricking in the kitchen,
taking less than a minute to slice the skin off a chicken.

killing the golden orbs

when we moved in
they were everywhere:
bannered uncountably between trees
or brocaded
among ferns and flowers,
tying their own luck like a Chinese knot
bodies and legs finicky as lockets
on veranda rails,
shadows filigreed on tiles
jounced by the wind

their restless fretwork
confusing the distance between
near and far
almost always a handspan
away, the browngold
of antique bells or handles,
ringing
into view at the last moment
or else they've ascended
and crown the footpaths
or forbid us
from certain doors,
lost in their gloss

when I kill them all
it is neighbourhood treason —
the mulchy woman who genuflects
in the scrub by our back fence
crunches distaste in her throat
my farm-born friend
unfurls her careful smile
my father belts down the phone

do you know they eat
all the other bugs do you like
roaches and moths
do you want your new house
full of insects
and while I hold the phone
to my ear Sam lopes
over the veranda and knocks
what bodies he can to the ground
and mourns them
they aren't poisonous
and won't come inside what
have you done

I rinsed
their webs in poison
after it was over I sneezed
and watched their long deaths
how they writhed
and died in air

I sat and allowed it
not doing less or more
later the rain came stressing down
a study in momentum
and even the highest of them fell
but this morning
new webs
which I must now attend to

Scott Cam helps me fix a few things around the house

Tell me about your private school days.
How about a trade: I'll give you mates rates
for my public school stories that match
your flannelette shirts. Scott Caminetti, show me
how to trim back my name.

Tell me a story
about growing up by the beach.
Whittle me a coffee table from the tree
of knowledge, teach me bandsaw from handsaw,
bark from firewood.

Scotty, can you mow my lawn? My father did it
'til I was twenty-three, then he moved interstate.
Scotty, I need new locks on all the doors.
I've heard you're an expert on pets:
do you know how to stop geckoes mating
on the ceiling or how to poison
the neighbour's lonely dog
whose crying excites the cockatoos?

Scotty, how do you repair the body?
Do your best: fix my cracking knees,
brush and trim my hair. I've got a cavity
but I won't go to the dentist.
So good luck with that.

Read to me from *The Waste Land*.
When you're done, I've got these pictures to hang.
How cheap can art be
before it's no longer refined? Now listen:
tell me if this line scans.

Crescent Road

3 p.m. The hour of housecats whiskering
across open-palmed backyards
while cars shark up this hill

much too fast.
The road's a double nothing: it splits
into tarry hoops of cul-de-sacs

that slingshot all cars
back the way they came.
In passenger seats

people shake their maps like babies.
Nobody comes here
who is not lost or home.

6 a.m. The sun's barely a blister
on the horizon's thumb and a runner,
new to town, chisels

up the street,
meets the club foot of one dead end.
Back at the fork, lactic patches

on his high-vis legs,
he tries downhill and gets
nowhere again.

Twice in a row and he believes he's arrived
in some nightmare town
which he now fears

he might never escape. The highway,
close enough to burr in the ear,
promised him order

but here he's mazed
in these two ends, bent
on staying dead.

genius loci

god of wrong-coloured curtains we kept anyway
god of the chlorine-poisoned geckoes and treefrogs
in the filter box god of pale brown spiders that cruise
humid cupboards empty shoes a sleep-warm bed
god of cups exiled to drink up dust
pens that should be thrown out
laundry baskets losing their handles
god of half-closed eyes in photographs
god of the oilslick chests of male wrens
and the jenny wren cowled in brown
god of foxes and feral cats thumbing through scrub
god with the patience of a skink growing back its tail
god of lights left on all night
god of wind that carries off plastic chairs
and elbows through thatches of trees
god that stands behind the locked door and looks out

2

A history of blue

Brainscan blue of the horizon's edge
before dawn. That is the blue
of indecision. Five blue lights blinking
the plane through metaldust sky
while the Pacific lilts like aquarium-plastic
around some humid or hypothermic blue latitude.
Look closer. Here's Stradbroke Island
in shades of blue-ringed octopus,
blackblue crabs on rocks like moving bruises.
Drowsy blue of my teetotal grandfather's tattoo
and the blue book of his brain
that remembers all birds by their Latin names.
Blue guts of swimming pools, blue-tongues
scrummed in one shady corner. First and last:
the sky's huge blue hand pressed
against the windows.

Buying satin dresses at Yu Garden

I buy them like fruit,
my body

still on the bike,
one foot grounded.

This one like a wedge
of lime on my lip.

Idiot machines
clench these colours

together in some grainy
province,

craft
ravelled down

to whatever thread's
cheapest, raw cord

around the waist,
three cuts: head, arms.

This one slides
from its hanger, a ripe

weight in my hand,
crazed yellow strung

from the machine's
tropic mind.

The street slings past.
A man pushes

his fruit cart, calls out.
I lay the dress

in my basket, hand over
blanched banknotes,

and though I know
this appetite can't be met

by a dress
it is so delicious

that both my feet
are already off the ground.

Alla prima

He is still the stillest hand, sure
that all terrors are palm-sized,
can be cupped against the chest
like a chick
to slow its tapping heart.

He eats the pale heart
of a lettuce, grates unpeeled
carrots into stew, chews
stalks, sucks flowers,
pronounces all vowels the same.
Marks his page
with odd leaves. Leaves
marks on screens.

The conch-curl of his right hand,
one steel-pinned finger
soldered in a rough crescent.
He rolls messy cigarettes and lets
the smell sprawl over him,
his beard-burred skin.

A grip that catches
at cock, cat, toe, book, smoke,
tumbler of scotch
on the rocks. Broke the backbone
of Nietzsche's *Complete Works*,
spattered it with notes
and now that sour German face
erodes beside his bed.

The map-blue sound of his voice lapping
in the phone's clear cup.
He speaks me to sleep.
Says, this will make you happy,
and it does.

On luck

I have been wondering
if it's bad luck
to write a love poem
for you

when others
that began like this
had to end so that I could be
here, listening
to you breathe as you sleep.

Even now
you are holding my body
with both hands.

I think you would tell me
it is not bad luck.
You would say,
let's walk down to the river
and have breakfast.

scaffolding

shang   hai   means
up river   or up
from the sea
        or above sea   level
either   I am   not fluent
or   nobody says it
the same way

there's no   conjugating verbs
in mandarin
sometimes   I have
no sense of tense
and then   all sorts of things
        spill:

so I am still   hauling
my heavenblue bike
        up twenty stairs
to my apartment   at three a.m.—
which is not unusual
        in shang   hai
        it seems safe
to be   female
and alone
                except some cases
                you hear of;
                some people you don't
                        ever see
—at three a.m. in the sepia wash
        of beer
I see that the first floor neighbours
        have started to renovate

bamboo scaffolding
is crocheted
around their   doorways

it is hard to describe
this building
and to say why I can see
        that a rat
glossing past   me on the stairs
                              has snuck into
        the halfbuilt kitchen
and fit itself into a cupboard
        sleek as an   appliance

in the morning   going
        down again   my bike
        chainsaws
through   a ruck of metal
and snapped bamboo

all day I skim
from place to place
        seeking the end
of the city
which has no suburbs
and   burns
    like a sun on its own dense fuel
the skyline is   revised
        daily
and the census is probably   wrong

wherever I ride
there is   more
                scaffolding

shang   hai   is   a dream
  I had I left
some things   there
I might
        not   go back   for them

the neighbours
are still
        not finished

Pomegranate

It's winter and she has grown
so thin. She is cutting a pomegranate,
which some dissolved lover bought
and left in her apartment
along with a few other things—reading
glasses, a library book that sits
above the television accruing fees, radiant
with dust. As she cuts she tells me
that today her tape measure
recoiled and sliced the flesh
of her palm while she measured
a client's kitchen for an island bench.
I darken our glasses with more wine
and imagine each yellow inch
rattling across a stranger's
floorboards, the nick of shock
in her throat before she stood again
and asked for a towel. She says he gave
her a few tissues and an address
to which she could email the quote.
The pomegranate rolls on either side
of her knife, two halves
wobbling like dollars about to fall,
and inside them hardness
and clots of colour that redden
the bandage on her palm.
She is almost through
the dark half of this year.

Meteorology

I can predict the future. A little. And everyone loves
to talk about the weather. I find what patterns I can, stay
a day or two ahead of what's happening. Sometimes it's hail,
a rash of red light on the display screens. Flattening wind –
that's blue and white, much like in real life. I love the way
rain's called *showers*, which implies comfort.
Of course it's not an exact science. You trust the sky
to tell the truth and then find that it lied.
Here's a beach, here's a nor'easter polishing
the ocean. Sometimes I think of all that air piled on us,
how it pushes us down. It's what keeps us here. Weather's never
late or early, never feels distant or overly rehearsed.
Some nights I watch the man who delivers it to camera.
He took a special course to learn to move in reverse.

Limit Philosophy

At parties I'm always excusing myself
by saying I don't want to talk about Nietzsche.
In Sils Maria the glib bells are probably ringing
and I don't want to talk about Nietzsche.
I hate it when the plane reaches 33,000 feet
and the pilot delivers his report on Nietzsche.
When tonight's broadcast is brought to you by
Nietzsche and there's been rising violence
in Nietzsche, when some ballots got lost
and by default we elected Nietzsche,
or when all the drinks come and mine is the one
with too much Nietzsche. I can't sleep
for noticing my partner's Nietzschean grammar,
the wilful tilt of his chin, the huge O! of his body
when we climb out of bed into cold air.
Here is a fable I tell myself: there were two friends
who lived at the top of a mountain
and neither had ever heard of Nietzsche.

Backcountry

He will never punctuate, be punctual, have change
for the bus or remember the name of the man
who wrote *Wake in Fright*. His brain earthquakes
from one place to the next and gives me no rest —
he leaves his card in cash machines,
lost the only known copies of his first two degrees.

Now he is asleep, laying the weird wreath
of his breath on my back.
Last night he walked for hours in his mind's backcountry,
jangled the bedroom light in my eyes
at half past three. He spends hours noosed in a nightmare
feet off the bed, toeing air, always shirtless, sweating,
a body that stored years of heat from fruit-picking
at the rim of some mine-split town.

He spits in the bin, leaves tobacco scribbled
over desks and benches. The blunt axe
of his cough chops his body and he wakes
to the simplest colour: the sun a minor light,
wind itching the eucalypts. Then remembers
wet clothes he should have put on the line.

He says he feels his age snapping its fingers
in his spine and lies prone
over the bed's scuttled bones: he can't lift things
anymore, but forgets. His past is tarred
with payment-plan fines, debtors stringing calls
across oceans to find him.

My favourite wineglasses
each spent their last seconds an inch
from the back of his wrist. Then the decadent

crash and a weeklong crystal silt
on the floor. And when he wakes
late, afternoon already turned umber,
all I can offer is inertia:
my cold back, spiked
like an echidna.

the ferret population of shanghai: some anecdotal evidence

my friend says ferrets
roam the streets
they were released a long time ago
to catch rats   or perhaps it was
roaches   he says
now they thrive in back alleys and stairwells
        the thresholds of people's lives

he says they're called   yòu
or perhaps it's   māo yòu
and you can see them at night
on sinan lu   where dozens of men
are re-cladding the houses

most mornings workers drip
like melting ice from the neocolonial eaves
hanging neon signs in english
the old tenants   shuttled
to some outer orbit

i am doubtful
of most of my friend's stories
and of this loose grip
on language: mine
                       and his

either way
the rats and roaches are still out there
but some nights riding
home late
I think I see   white ferrets
            streaming

under the gates
and into those houses
where nobody is allowed to live

Snore

I take it personally. This thing
clawing in your throat
has no place in a speaking world.
It seesaws on some huge
rusted hinge or is wrenched
like a tin roof
in a house-wrecking wind.
Outside, the moon persists
with its one white vowel,
while beside me the sound
drags out half-dead and foreign
as Latin in the bedroom's air.
I stay curled on this island
where the sound shreds all maps
and flares and flares
in black light, dressed in phlegm,
howling for a fight.

Sleep Paralysis

You're stuck
tongue to lung
and the thing
that's got your breath
trapped in
is smooth as a stone.
You can't break its skin.
Your limbs are absent,
throat glassed shut,
body pared back
to one strip
of thought,
the white cuticle
of terror.
Then some old crowcall
in your bones
brings you back.
Your body comes unlocked
and you hang
each thought
carefully as a painting,
unfurl the shivery links
of one hand,
open both eyes
to blue light
and outside a cold
evening smell
rises from the grass
like a breath.

Batfish

North Stradbroke Island

We have tried all the activities: fishing, lying
in the sun with our faces shaded by books,
listening to tarps batwing in the wind.

We've talked. We've ignored each other.
Across the water: ferries and jetskis, fishermen
at the Amity Point jetty, where a fat dolphin snaps

every underweight catch they try to throw back.
In boots, I go down to the mangroves
where batfish babies on their sides

dream of being a dead leaf. Like all children, the force
of their belief is strong, but it fails. I see one,
given away by the caviar-drop of its eye.

It won't laze here forever. Grown up, it forgets
this shallow light and sinks itself. This whole time,
it's been thinking of where it will go.

Storage

Every few years
I find myself crisped
to a mothwing
in a garage
or in the whiteblue carapace
of a dress stippled with tiny holes.

Who eats these pieces?
What hunger am I
seeing through,
held up to the light,
after all these years?

The Brooklyn International Motel

Oily light in the corridors
and the smell of old suitcases
we borrowed from your parents.

You write our room number
on the back of your hand, spread
postcards on rough carpet.

Through the louvers
we watch emergency lights flash,
dragging cars out of fog.

Later, in the dark, you search for the bed.
Crookedness
meets your fingertips.

You grip my bent leg
like a branch
to climb up and sit on.

In other rooms,
people wait for hot water with a hand
in the shower.

From these windows
the world looks nothing like itself.
The ceiling has stolen some low stars.

Across the Pacific
the battered poinciana still stands
outside the house we live in.

Come closer.
The slow roll of cities
will turn us home soon.

Ways to suffer

On a yacht, drinking bellinis in a yellow robe.
By torchlight, in the garden, looking for your keys.
By overstaying your welcome.
By moving house in January.
At night or in the day. Either will work.
If at night, you can lie flat on your back and wonder if the front door
    is locked.
If during the day, there are many places to start: busses, press
    conferences, complexes
for the ageing, poor, detained, dead.
In the company of drunks, who always sit in sour weather.
Beside a sliced onion, which will soak up your suffering so you won't
    bear it alone.
By becoming a witch; by becoming a celebrity; by becoming a public
    school teacher.

Be awake between two and three a.m.
Order the seafood surprise or the house chardonnay.
Order spaghetti on the first date.
If you're on holiday: join the end of the line at Les Catacombes; swim
    at Bondi; get an eye
infection at Buñol; accept a glass of baijiu.
If at home: get involved in your local community,
in politics,
in a conversation about politics
with someone more educated than you.
Read your emails after two weeks away.
Read the comments section.
Read Dostoyevsky.
Don't read Dostoyevsky.
Talk to your friend who has recently seen a complicated play.
Drink with your friend who bottles her own beer.
Drink eight martinis the night before a disciplinary hearing.

Like Job, first on your knees, then demanding answers from the
    highest authority.
Like Thomas More, on principle, and in silence.
Like a fish trying to mimic the dead safety of a leaf.
Like a hermit crab with no bigger shell.
Like your father who checks every lock twice and twice again.
Like your mother who helps him out of love and pity.
Like you, watching them or turning away.

3

Tax return

If I call for help I am answered
by a voice swinging down from the clouds
or the floors above. My signature sprawls
in its too-small box. Days of tearing paper
with my teeth. Forms accumulate. I write in all caps
to make myself seem larger than I am.
Always one question I can't work out,
an extra expense to declare: I start giving myself
new names and addresses, a holiday
in the Whitsundays, I start to suspect
I bought a Lexus this year — I write it down
for safety's sake, begin tallying every dead
pen I've binned. It's never enough. I add in
my phone bill. My floorboards. My multivitamin.
Forms like cliffs that may collapse
under my weight. Still they accumulate
while years fold and fade like receipts.

air quality index

one of the last known plagues,
smog rides in
       with a cold front
first in the sky, then the back
                of the throat
     brings on bad
tempers, smothers us like a sweaty palm
    or a rag
           in the mouth

each morning daguerreotyped
     on my eyes:
     flash of brassy light, then curtains
        clinched together

heaters chafe
     all day in cafes
men poach in the great grey sheaves
    of their coats,
stutter emails while soda purrs
              over gin

towers inch
    out of sepia fog
cats stand on the brown brink
       of their shadows
   as cabs drift behind their lights
       and in backseats
passengers crack
     like knuckles
        in double-thick jackets

it delivers us back
            to a bronze age:
the godless power
                        tools abandoned
and across the river –
      crusted with coal boats
                  and iceless all winter –
factory workers are sent
                  home, fractured
like ice just dropped
                  in a drink

The snapping turtle

My friend delivered it as he left for Spring Festival,
drenching me in red gifts, flimsy New Years' luck.
The shell was sharp in places, soft where stamps
of moss were stuck. It looked like an evil
stone, an ancient treasure. I wanted to pry it apart
and keep what was hidden for myself.

Turtles know how to survive sharp falls, predators,
nature's wild swerves into ice or heat or rain.
They are unfazed by apocalypse. Outside,
fireworks wisecracked and my neighbours drank
with their families or scraped towards hometowns
on packed trains. All week I made and remade
our bed, paired socks that didn't belong, kept
the still turtle in my pocket or beside me while I slept.

ReSpimask

People always tell me Shanghai's not real
China, not *real* China as stadiums burst
open like volcanic craters and the neon strata
of freeways double and triple. I hear
they're building a beach in the calcified streets
of North Jiading. Twenty-seven new metro stations
opened this year, all sides of the city strapped
with tracks. Lately I feel myself sinking
like an office tower, some days I feel tall and taut
as a crane under floodlights. The view
from the Pearl Tower's clotted with smog
but only at sunset or when there's a queue.
I hear they've got plans in place to clear the air,
purifiers in every store, and today I saw new ReSpimasks
that come in patterns called Arctic, Cobalt
Venus, Hummingbird, Lightning and Paradise.

Assumption

after the Master of the Amsterdam Death of the Virgin (c. 1500)

This is the room
a rational mind lives in:
three cushions on a bench,
one window,
the brief white spines
of fire.

By the bed, apostles lick fingers
over each turn of the page.
They are twelve miraculous itineraries:
proof that all cities
are less than three days
from this room.

Eel-eyed, they gawk and mourn,
speak and lean,
candling sadness on their knees.
Their looks slide off her sallow face.
In all the books
she gently falls asleep
but here insomnia
shakes its purse under her eyes.

Perhaps she will stay
one more night in this bed,
expecting the sun
to appear in the curtains.
The bedroom door is open
because this is just someone's house.
People are passing by outside.
A dog stares in from the street.

Backyard occult

The problem is not
how to decipher an omen,
it's how to choose one.
Example: you see two crows
on a wire, then a man
who sneezes brutally
on the footpath behind you.
A black station wagon
tailgates you home. Rain
stencils the windows
of your bedroom. A crane
lunges over the house
next door. Floors above
you, someone plays
Clair de Lune on loop.
And all night you ask yourself:
which is it?

Bush stone-curlew

In another life you'd be at the theatre,
a brittle soprano smashing champagne
flutes on your way to stage.
Or at the edges of parties, nicking
canapes and leaving late, your gilt iris
brash in the cab's backseat.
But in this life you're understudy
to gaunt paperbarks and mynahs,
stalking your still self
in lakes and ground-floor windows,
an escaped Giacometti.
At night the mirrors of the world
switch off. You approach someone's stunned
backyard and take your voice from its box.

Mighty helpful

Scott Cam makes spaghetti for dinner again.
Scott Cam scrapes paint off the front door when he moves in.
Scott Cam smokes despite the body corporate policy.
Scott Cam drinks IPAs only if they're cheap.

Scott Cam hasn't vacuumed for a month,
hasn't taken out the bins. He parks
in the middle of the double garage.
He says he didn't poison the neighbour's cat
but I know he did.

Scott Cam never gets the washing in;
can't fold clothes straight or replace the cap
on the toothpaste. He eats peanut butter
with his fingers and doesn't rinse out
his tuna tins.

He watches trash. He leaves the door
unlocked, loses his keys. Let's not talk
about the bathroom. He definitely broke
the washing machine. Scott Cam airs
his problematic opinions,
sometimes says *bitch* and pretends
it's a joke.

Two Paintings by Jan van Eyck

Madonna in the Church (1438)

How did she get in? She's sixty
feet tall and carrying a monstrous
child. Does she get to take off that crown,
to put down the boy, the cloak?

Outside it's summer,
stained glass splices the brickwork
around her, her crown has not yet
dropped a single jewel. She's persevering

with metaphor, and with benevolence
towards those two gawkers in back.
She's probably done
with angels, the green watermelon rind
of their wings.

On hot nights when I get home late,
I think of her standing still in that cathedral
as I take off my shoes, my clothes,
feel my body slipping back

into its former shape. Then I stand
in the shower
and let water fall and fall
over my raised face.

The Arnolfini Portrait (1434)

Well, I have married a living venom-gland.
One of his first gifts was a fake dog,
which he had the taxidermist make –
it's as good as a real one,
if not better. Look into its glass eyes
and you see yourself. Also these sandals,
a little painful, hard to stand or run.
I've kicked them off.

The round mirror spinning Christ's
passions behind me –
that was another of his gifts,
the glass beads, his, all his.

This morning I saw it was still
summer, the cherries hung on, oranges
rolled and rolled on the windowsill
but never fell.
I entered the greenhouse
of my gown.

Here's the thing: he moves
so quietly, room to room. Just before
the master arrived to paint
our picture, I'd found myself caught
in the lock of his look
in that mirror.

Like many poisonous things, some parts of him
are beautiful. You should have seen
the trim waist on our wedding night.
And his pale shoulders whetting
their blades on moonlight.

In the Shanghai Museum

9.01 am

The world will be here
soon. I eye off a scribe's
chair, wonder
what's left
of his ancient brain.
Can it be cupped
in the palm? Is it crisp?

I imagine it curved
in on itself, ingrown
like a toenail,
flesh scrunched pinkly
around it.

In this image
the men are all calligraphy:
their gowns scrolled
behind glass.

Knocked off
or lost.
A thousand years
in a case is no way
to spend history.

The trick
is not to count
the minutes.

Outside in People's Park
old men practice characters
on pigeon-flecked cement,
arm-length brushes
dipped in water.

When I get home
I check the news
in case
a dynasty has fallen.

At the pet market, hunting for luck-monkeys

I heard they sell luck in its purest forms here:
marmosets the size of your finger, a goshawk snibbed
to an iron bar, the odd fennec fox, gold
pufferfish that hang like hieroglyphs.
I slip through aisles of vicious crickets,
eyeing their cages' wicker hinges.
Some are lucky, some aren't. I can't tell
which is which: each has muscles
like thick black twine, fine manes of thigh-hair.
At ankle-height everything's translucent
or plain – dumb guppies, snake-lunch mice
pacing sawdust while just above,
gerbils roll soft as blessings into pink and blue boxes.
Turtles on every surface, piled in glass bowls
like business cards, decades-old turtles by the cash
registers, still as icons, snapping turtles rigging
their jaws open. White crays stir for scraps
in the filter's shirred water, a loose cat drifts a paw
among the angelfish – none of it's enough.

It's the portable marmoset I want:
palm-sized, tame, glib lipless face, the cure
for a luckless year. Instead I find chipmunks
cartooning around, mating upside down
at the back of the market, where crowds don't come.
Here: shabby rabbits, teenage dogs too big for their cages,
revealing the secret that pets grow
old and slow. Nobody wants an animal that ages.
Back out front, a dead cichlid will never hit tank-bottom:
six others buoy her up with their mouths.
When I need luck, I'll take whatever's on sale:
songbird, fat cricket, thumb-monkey.

Flat Earth Theory

I can't believe in a spherical earth. We move
rung by rung. Stars like a spray of spit
between terse tangents of planets. Nerves
in their new-shoelace neon have a start and end,
linear as logic. Laid on our backs, we can trawl blood
from foot to brain to recover from a faint.
And whatever slow turns the planet makes aren't part
of some larger reasoning: the earth's blue zero
carried over while meteors glance us in the dark.
We were afraid in our beds but that time has passed.
Weather never repeats. Each year we revise our vocabulary
of storms: this summer there was sleet where we laid
our towels on the beach. Rain does not recognise itself
in puddles, does not give birth or die. It moves on.
We are not coming back to any place.

Pigeon

I love it when a pigeon or sparrow
or some other bird
nobody wants to photograph or save
from extinction
walks into a shop
and instead of instantly realising
that it can't afford anything,
it continues to pace forward,
which is especially good in pigeons,
whose oil-rainbowed necks are thick
and flexible, as if custom-made
for browsing.

I think if teenagers
behind the counters didn't get so excited
and chase them away,
the birds might enjoy an hour or two
among the clothes racks,
or smelling the life-giving smell
of fresh sandwiches.
One of the best moments
of my life
occurred yesterday morning
at my favourite
bakery, when I met the gold eyes
of the pigeon who was standing on the counter
above the meat pies,
tilting her head to ask what I would like.

R.S.V.P.

Gertrude Stein, I'd gratis all my Picassos to be left alone
on a Saturday night, to never entertain guests at home.

I'd rather spill wine on someone else's linens
and leave as late or early as I pleased.

I'm suspicious, Gertrude Stein, of people who love company —
be an auctioneer if you're so keen on crowds.

Who'd want to spend days chatting, knee to knee
with friends who think dinner means a long weekend?

Artists accumulate like knickknacks. You set them up
by the oven, with your lamps and porcelain chickens.

You ration your wit. You pray for your cook.
You write, if you can, in the thick part of night.

Who'd endure a room full of men, their goatees
and eyes like thrown stones? You would,

Gertrude Stein: in photos you flatten the foreground
with your smile. Even your brooch

could win an argument, your Ford could survive
the wrong side of any road.

Who'd dare ask you to leave the house
if you wanted to stay on for drinks after dinner?

auction

I've seen the   AUCTION   sign wilting all   summer
today is the first   perfectly cool day: wind rinses leaves
        from fig-trees   I am lush   with laziness   listening in bed
to a man's   brylcreem speech   vault   across the road
I can't hear   the words   but I know this   is a scene   from tv:
the auctioneer's teeth   flacking like banners   neighbours
out for   some topical banter then   the hammer
of his hand as   bids pitch up   like thrown styrofoam
in the chill   morning wind that will   smooth us into june
        the house holds still   while leaves wash   against broken windows
then it's over   applause for the new owners   who flip
signatures on paperwork   behind them wind cuffs   the house
        its edges sharpen   in flensing light
and only now they can see   how much work   must be done

4

Hotel del Coronado

The past is so easy to photograph.
A facade, a moss-flecked sign. Gulls fling
into wind. The hotel surrenders
to background while you hold my coat
out of frame, sand on your boots. You tell me
the hotel still opens in summer.
Ten minutes ago I read it on a sign.
The Pacific recycles itself, contributes nothing.
We stand under balconies and can't see inside
to the armoires and carpets, four-posters
where presidents held paperbacks to lamplight.
My hands are cold, always cold.
My merciless twenties: nothing pleases me.
I turn towards your truck. Above it, a mute bird
falls and rises into distance. You want to stop
for ice-cream, beer, a postcard; anything
to alleviate this. Everything's closed.
We circle in blank wind. The hotel
looks the same from every angle.

Weekday lizard sketches

1

Perhaps I am the only one
who sees the baby water dragons
step into a racket of sun
on Monday afternoons:
three o'clock, the rest
of the world at work.

2

Two favourite kinds of skinks:
one's brown and benign,
sometimes fattening around
the middle, the other's grey-striped,
thinner, the bravado of a much
bigger creature. A grey one hangs
from my fingertip
by its ludicrous mouth.

3

Look how the lace monitor
rests vertical on a scribbly gum,
half an eyelid from non-existence.
Still, people swerve off the path
and snatch up their toddlers.
If I throw chicken scraps,
it adjusts the gold disc
of its eye, descends.

4

When I was a child I poured
skinks in a bucket,
showered them with grass
and snapped sticks, then bolted off.
Days later, found crisps
of skin, ants rivering
in and out of the eyes. Dispensed
a measure of tears, caught more.

5

My whole life there has been
a blue-tongue not far off.
The cool weight of its look hinges
me to these weekday mornings —
hanging my few shirts
on the line while the sun
rings through my blood.

The Curator at St. Bavo's Cathedral, Ghent

after the Ghent Altarpiece, by Jan van Eyck (1432)

I've been coming here
since I was a child.
You should have seen the hordes
of restorers last year.
They came with lasers, cameras
and a man from the *New Yorker*.

I watched behind glass
with half the town as they bore
down on it, shearing
wood and glue, working back to front.

Stand just here. Look: he gives us
Mary as someone's bookish sister,
involved in a novel she can't put down,
and see how the lamb on its dais
has perfect aim:
the parabola of blood spouting
from chest to chalice
is the purest physics.

The apostles always come when called
and are on the approach, stalked
by the Pope and his retinue.
To your right: you can't miss St. Christopher,
who loves a working holiday,
and is twice the size
of the other folks. Perhaps he's grown
in proportion to his time spent in leisure.

The centuries have failed
to humble Eve.
She refuses to cover the black chaff
at her groin with one hand
and in the other she's holding
an insubstantial apple,
so sullen she can barely stand.

Now, the judges: someone's sweet brown horse
turns to hold our gaze,
but his master's face
says they're running late.
The man beside him knows it, back
already turned on pale castles
blooming like lamplight
far off in the forest.
On the whole – disapproval.

No wonder this is the panel they stole.
How can we look away
from the sheep's utter confidence, green fields
where the water of redemption runs
down the grass towards us,
to this plain chaos.

Look, it's about to happen
right there at the edge of the frame:
one judge's horse has caught her foot
on a rock. Her tongue drags in air,
and any moment she'll raise up
her dove-white body
and everything will begin
to disintegrate.

Rabindranath Tagore appears in Lismore, NSW

Today, jetlagging
through this hemisphere's
tar-melt afternoon
in the weatherboard library, I find
between pleated copies of Rilke
and Yeats, the *Collected Poems and Plays*
of Rabindranath Tagore,

whose bust surveys the corner
of my street in Shanghai,
his green plinth strange and lovely
on its slope of ageless flowers.

It is as if I am back on that wishbone
of road in the city I have just left:
he faces the yóutiáo stall
where I'd stand in line
on Sunday mornings,

and each week, repeating xièxiè
as I took the crisp dough,
I would turn towards home
and meet my eyes
in his eyes.

Fruit flies

They speck my vision like dead
pixels, the kitchen blurred by moving static:
fruit flies gravelling the apples, adventuring
in wineglasses where they drown
in rich merlot like kings. Bananas I bought
a day ago have already begun to split their skins
and call more fruit flies in. Clear sight
is winter's luxury, the bin a dry white square,
the sink's crisp void. Now the black-lipped
benchtops cannot hold still. The sink
runs with them. All outlines reduced to estimate.
Hazed windows in the flyblown sun.
Kill them all. More will come.

Our apartment in Shanghai has three rooms

137 Nanchang Rd

1.
Practicing sleep by your side,
I lie, chew tongue-muscle,
cheek and jaw,
eye off dawn.

Split curtains where the white-rust sky
saws through.
Long hours of half-light;
thirteen ways
of staring at a blank screen.

2.
I eat strawberries, throw tops
onto neighbours' roofs
while you read Bashō
in a spoonful of sun.

Lines on a palm, a handful
of scratches from plants
someone before us
left dead in their pots.
We haven't uprooted them
or planted something new.

3.
You dig holes under shrubs,
stub your cigarettes
on their scrambled roots.

I clear the scrum of beer bottles
and honey-crisp crusts
stuck to yesterday's paper.

Scraps of a day spent
trawling these floorboards,
which my father told me
are rare, haven't been used
in apartments
for years.

I start hammering
back
to before we lived here.

Varnish

Each night they sleep with the amber
smell of varnish
in their moonscraped room

as floors soak under brief
sheets of wind. Light slicks
across the stacked kitchen chairs.

When they wake to soak the split timber
again they slip through hours like water
or sleep, they forget it is neither – perhaps

weeks have passed and now they are varnish
or animal or neither, pouring
through hours, fine as sugar,

waking to soak the split timber
again. When they sleep
the floor becomes clear as water or melts

in the centre, they are not sure
how much longer they must eat and sleep
while soaked in amber. Furniture is formless

under drop sheets, more animal than water
neither remembers the order
it goes in. This is what the mind

wants to know at three a.m.:
how many days does it take
to paint wood the colour of wood?

major foundation repairs

late afternoon   light slides
                              like olive oil
in the mind's   hot corners
                                  citronella
                                  a tin of almost-warm soup
your phone's dead   again
                                  one remaining
        power point   throttled
        by the fluorescent

        that bar of   light
                        is what   your mind
        returns to : the single image
        of these   mosquito-trimmed evenings

a glass of wine might lash you
                          to the mattress
                              and for a few
                              raw hours you dream
of yourself   crawfishing
                      through the rooms   of this house
                      your hand   is a tool
                              or a claw
                      you nip off   every light
daring the house to sear you   into darkness
                              for good
                              this time

Letters addressed to Jan van Eyck's *Portrait of a Man*

Jan, why didn't you just call it
Self-Portrait? I sat today and looked at the tree
where wrens flinched branch to branch.
I had nothing to say about it.
I sat there for hours.
How was it for you after Hubert
died and they called you to finish
the altarpiece he'd begun? What did you do,
facing its oak-wood wings,
with bits of paint he'd already laid?
I want your opinion, not 'second in art'.
My arse. How did you know when to start again?
I'm sorry you missed your brother.

Jan, today I saw a king parrot.
You'd have liked it. Europeans
understand green. You understood it more
than most: John's robe
in your altarpiece; the litter
of milk thistle on the ground.
You must have stood so close to the wood,
your brushes with just one or two hairs.
Those cliffs like real geography.
Had Hubert done enough, had he started
something you wanted to finish?
I don't think you liked answering questions.
Your self-portrait allocates itself
no expression. All those angels
laughing, the faithful furrowing
their brows, heavy-lidded merchants
who were clearly out to kill for a bolt
of cloth — those were for others.
Your own face tells us only

what it is to hold back. Nothing else.

Jan, let's agree that art is hopeless.
So is history. You can wear that red chaperon
to the end of time and it won't help.
Well, I cleaned out the rooms,
threw out the boots and hats,
changed sheets. It was quick.
You must have woken in the strict
Bruges winter, Hubert
gone, summer gone, your workshop
beaded with grey light,
and reached a decision.
Tell me how to arrange
a plain look on my face, how to go on
without giving away
anything I need.

Monopoly

1. Kent Road, Wooloowin

the landlord sold in under a fortnight.
took us by surprise. we packed up
and rented a place on the same street.

stuffed in three rooms, we transplanted the fridge
from kitchen to deck, still full of milk
and ice-fringed packs of weekday meat.

it sat for weeks on the whitening timber,
collecting ants in its chilled coils.
splinters nibbed our bare feet

when we came out each morning
for eggs or jam. it hummed
through umber afternoons when heat

thickened air to wax, until in december
we took a holiday and a circuit snapped
off the power for a week.

on the deck when we came back: masses
of flies and neighbourhood cats; meat
seething in the dark freezer.

2. Vine Street, Clayfield

in this house we liked to doze under breezes
in the hammock-hung yard
while inside kitchen chairs stewed

in bedrooms, cutlery in vases lined the windows
and sent circles of light roaming the walls
like tiny gold animals. our dishwasher, trailing its cords

in the laundry, disgorged a wet plug of gunk
like an afterbirth, which we ignored.
we washed clothes day-to-day

in the kitchen sink, lived
with shirts hanging like colourful ghosts
in windows and doorways

3. Bond Street, West End

we signed the lease, moved everything in,
future tensed through unpacked rooms:
imagine a deck; imagine a pool.

fluorescents cleansed us with astringent light
as we unwound snares of plugless cords. fleets
of old batteries tacked and jibbed under our feet.

light fittings shattered like wineglasses
in our hands, releasing the mild rain of a decade's
dead moths. we nabbed a cheap lounge

and, like mafia bosses, happily snapped its legs off.
we circled the bedroom with its sliding
doors and mirrors to the floor. so much

still to do, but there we saw ourselves for the first time
in a year: you were a thimble and I was a wheelbarrow.
nobody wins on just rent and chance.

hallways

you pace out your relationship
to the State in the hallways of every
hospital and school
hallways are tunnels from the enlightenment's
pristine logic space to think
between acts
points of arrival or departure
antimetaphysical and entirely precise

in rooms objects and people
are static their presence is intentional
or it is not this is signified
by their proximity to the hallway
history is about who controls hallways
the medici villas were stented
with hallways for transporting
rumours and cash

science fiction depends
on hallways to make spacecraft
seem believable because hallways
lead somewhere other than the infinite
people need hallways to survive places
the problem with Bentham's Panopticon was
not enough hallways where else does the guard
step away from the inmate's
ruined face
it's always there where a madman
champs his axe or gun or just the bare
glint of hands and doesn't your lover
always live in a room at the end of a hallway
which turns out to be the same length

as the louche dream   you're having
you never quite get there
aren't you running   late every morning
down this endless hallway   where you gasp apologies
to your manager   for your sick child
or bald tyres
and when you're wheeled   to theatre
in an emergency   the hallway
is a funnel for the present   tense isn't it
always a hallway   you run down in nightmares
and even now
your childhood photo   hangs
at the end   of your parents'
hallway   so you see
your little   self
when you trawl   towards the bathroom
in the dark

dream clean

you are wise
to never leave a room
      empty-handed

      make it a point
to rotate your items
as they do in museums:
focus on just one format
      this could be   travel brochures
                                     cassettes
                                     greeting cards

for every item
      you bring home
get rid of two

make a list of everyone
      the children's teachers
      the housekeeper
      babysitter

make a habit of putting things
      in the space available
first it will require   a list

designate another room
for things pertaining
to the future   travel brochures
                         cassettes
                         greeting cards

stand back
from your things
ask yourself whether
you can see   yourself

       you may have to make
       a list
              they're inexpensive
              and comfortable
you may have
to make your bedroom
       your personal retreat

the past takes up
a huge amount of space

Huangshan sonnet

Dazed with mountain snow and anger I arrived at last.
I leapt from the train into the station's darkness. All afternoon
I'd stared through the window, past his unforgivable face,
at snow-blind houses, precarious cars, ice on the pass
far above. He kicked along behind me on the way into town
penitent or sullen, impossible to say. I loved to flay
him with inattention: blanket silence, clipped syllables,
sweeping his argument's pages to the ground.

Eventually we stopped to eat, ordered bottles of beer
and if our silence had been any less crisp, if I'd smiled
at a joke or let him draw me into a story, I'd have poured
half that beer down my throat when it came. Instead, my whole body
an accusation, I took one prim sip, then stopped to spit
a fine crescent of glass into his supplicating palms.

Insomnia Remedy

You need lashings
of lavender oil
on your pillow.

Dip your hair
in it. Mix
it with gin

and drink all
week. Soak your
lover until he

becomes a paperweight.
Then lay out
fresh white sheets.

Bond cleaning

You never get it all back. Not the whole bond,
not the days spent worrying with a sponge
at tidelines of dirt where you've toed the wall
behind your desk for years. You're shocked
at the messes you've made, the piles of paper
grown huge and useless, skirting boards cuticled
with your muck, you who've always been so clean.
The furniture shoved aside as though suddenly,
after years in the house, you can't get enough space.
Even your toes have betrayed you, the prints
of dirt behind the desk you didn't see yourself
making, guiltless as animal tracks. You want
to leave those marks. Without the desk
they could mean anything.

morning on some continents

i sweat in a guest room
                    and change
the sheets again   when i leave

our father who art
            in the backyard
sorry about   what happened
            to the trampoline

i unpack
            and pack   my body
into the standing mirror
            there i am

my clothes have all
                    grown larger
i am always   expanding

this morning it is february:
            cereal
                        tranquil
    in a new bowl

my narrow summer
            spent   glitching
                        through long-haul flights

shower at 3 a.m.
            in my parents' silent house
at 6 a.m.
            in my daylight apartment
at midnight

evening again   please
          let me sleep
for a few small hours

i am here
     in the future:
          this breakable house
with serene   pairs of lamps
and ceramic jars
is the house
          of my childhood
there i am   on the shining fridge
my handwriting
               on a postcard

the fridge spits cool water
a magpie tips   its throat
          toward morning

i unpack
               then pack again
spare keys still under
               a succulent

there i am   above the dining table
          throwing a softball
terrible aim
          not looking
               where i'm throwing

all day   the pacific's faint accent
          in the background
like a sleep
          recording

long seasons of   sky
                    fence   yard
rosellas shuffle
        their monopoly-money feathers
above the punctured
                trampoline

Notes

The poem 'ReSpimask' begins with a line from an earlier essay, published in *Westerly* 62.2, titled 'A mirror in the dark'.

Acknowledgments

Poems included in this manuscript have appeared in the following publications: *Ambit* (UK), *Australian Poetry Journal*, *Best Australian Poems*, *Cordite Poetry Review*, *foam:e*, *Griffith Review*, *Island Magazine*, *Mascara Literary Review*, *Meanjin*, *Meniscus*, *Peril*, *Plumwood Mountain*, *Southerly*, *SWAMP*, *Tincture Journal*, *Transnational Literature*, *Voiceworks* and *Westerly*. Some of the poems in this collection were written during a residency at Varuna, the Writers' House.

www.ingramcontent.com/pod-product-compliance
Lightning Source LLC
Chambersburg PA
CBHW030847090426
42737CB00009B/1132